SMARTASS ANSWERS TO Stupid INTERVIEW QUESTIONS

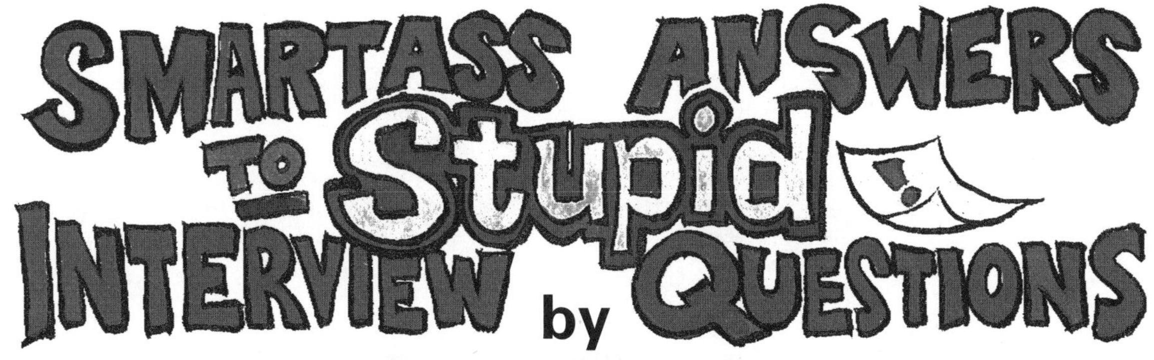

by
Barry Shamis

illustrated by
Sam Day

Leverage Press
Issaquah, WA

Smartass Answers to Stupid Interview Questions

Published by Leverage Press, Issaquah, WA

Disclaimer: the purpose of this book is to entertain. The author and Leverage Press shall have neither liability nor responsibility to any person or entity with respect to any loss or damage caused or alleged to be caused directly or indirectly by anyone silly enough to actually use this information in a real job interview.

Library of Congress Catalog Card Number 96-94735
Library of Congress Cataloging-in-Publication Data
Shamis, Barry.
Smartass answers to stupid interview questions / by Barry Shamis
p. cm.
ISBN 0-9653930-0-3

1. Employment interviewing—Humor. I. Title
HF5549.5.I6S43 1996 650.14
QBI 96–40238

Printed in the United States of America
01 00 99 98 97 96 5 4 3 2 1

Dedication

To all the tortured souls in the world
who have had to listen to silly interview questions …
this book is for you.

Contents

Acknowledgments

Writing a book is a team affair, and the team for this book is really special. Scott Pinzon of Pinpoint Marketing Communications has been invaluable editing and reviewing the content, as well as designing the layout. Sam Day's illustrations speak for themselves. Also, the people at Leverage Press have been great to work with.

They say that writing a book is like giving birth. Well, I'm tired of being pregnant ... just ask my family! I want to thank my wife and son for putting up with me in general, but especially during the writing of this book.

And finally, to all the people who have attended my presentations and shared with me your "special" questions ... thanks!

Foreword

Quick! Name something we all hate but do anyway!

No, we're not talking about that examination for prostate cancer, we're talking about interviewing for a job. This awkward process consists of one person who feels nervous and uncomfortable being asked questions by another person who usually feels just as uncomfortable.

You might be thinking, *Hey, why would the interviewer feel nervous? I'm the poor schmoe who has everything riding on the interview.*

The answer: most interviewers have no idea what they're doing.

Employees get promoted to management and then get told to hire people. Without guidance, they thrash around for an effective way to do it. Desperately, they pick up the latest book by some flavor-of-the-month corporate ju-ju doctor and read a lot of misinformation on the subject, which they believe wholeheartedly.

This is when the real trouble starts, and why some job interviews turn so strange.

How much bad advice has been written on how to conduct an effective job interview? So much that every question in this book came from a legitimate "expert" source such as a book, a seminar or an article. I did not make up even one question, not even that really ridiculous one on page 45.

With advice like this from the so-called experts, it's no wonder managers screw up job interviews and the process makes everyone's Top Ten Most Stressful Situations list. Interviews are stressful because when you are asked an idiotic, irrelevant question like, "If you could be any animal, which would you be?" you must battle the urge to slap someone into tomorrow and instead try to frame an answer that makes you sound interested and intelligent.

For the past seventeen years I have been traveling all over the nation, debunking stupid job interview myths and teaching managers how to select good people. Of the many serious things I have to say about interviewing, much of it boils down to common sense. Isn't it obvious that if you ask a stock boring question like "Where do you want to be in five years?" you're going to get a stock, prepared answer that reveals nothing about the candidate? After so much of that, you just can't help but laugh. And that's why I wrote this book: for fun.

Therefore, this book is for all of you who have had to sit across the table, pretending that the questions were well thought out and original. And if you're currently unemployed, facing job interviews right now, don't feel too bad. It could be worse.

You could be the one asking the questions.

I hope you have as much fun reading this as I had writing it.

Career

Q. Why should I hire you?

A. Because they say that you should always hire people who are better than you!

Q. What is the biggest mistake you have made in your career?

A. You mean other than agreeing to this interview?

Q. Where do you want to be five years from now?

A. As far away from you as possible.

Q. Where do you want to be ten years from now?

A. Even farther away from you!

Q. Why do you want this job?

A. So I can have a front for my more lucrative activities.

Q. What are your long-term career objectives?

A. To attain a position where I can work for global peace and happiness on earth—oh sorry, that was my Miss America acceptance speech.

Q. Do you want to be President of this company?

A. You've got yourself a deal! Shake!

Q. How much thought have you given to your future?

A. Enough to know I want to have one without you in it!

Q. What do you really want in life?

A. A set of headphones would be great right about now.

Q. Who has exercised the greatest influence on you?

A. Exercise? No, I don't exercise.

Personal

Q. When did you become an adult?

A. It began when hair started growing in places it had never been.

Q. What do you remember about your life as a child?

A. The courts promised to suppress all that after I turned eighteen. Why do you want to know?

Q. Tell me about your family.

A. My grandparents came over from the old country at the turn of the century. They had nothing more than the clothes on their back. After settling in the Hell's Kitchen area of New York, my grandfather got into the olive oil importing business. Are you sure you want all the details?

Q. What kind of behavior was discouraged or punished by your parents?

A. Peeing in my bed was discouraged. Peeing on my sister's bed was punished.

Q. Who is the boss in your family?

A. Let me call my wife and ask what I am allowed to say.

Q. Describe your relationship with your children.

A. They yell…I yell louder! Any questions?

Q. Who do you admire most in history?

A. The Three Stooges.

Q. Why?

A. Because when someone asked them a stupid question they smacked the idiot in the face!

Q. What traits did you adopt from each of your parents?

A. My mother taught me to be polite to those not fortunate enough to know when they are making a complete fool of themselves. My dad taught me to hunt inferior creatures.

Q. Who do you want to impress the most?

A. This woman I met in a bar the other night.

Q. What are you saying to me by the way you are dressed?

A. "I can be a dork just like you."

Q. If you were independently wealthy, what would you do with your time?

A. Make certain I never again had to listen to an inane question from an overbearing, under-educated wannabe who's a legend in his own mind.

Q. What have you done to prepare yourself for leadership?

A. When I was small, I used a magnifying glass to fry ants. That taught me how people act when they are confronted with a superior being.

Q. How do you see yourself 100 years from now?

A. Dust!

Q. What five or six adjectives best describe you?

A. Really, really, really, really, really, cool!

Q. What words best describe your personal style?

A. Just three: "Fan – Freakin' – Tastic!"

Q. What was the last book you read?

A. *A Beginner's Guide to Violence in the Workplace.*

Self Appraisal

Q. What can you say to reassure me that you are aggressive enough for this job?

A. Give me this job or I will kill you!

Q. How were you able to get promoted so quickly?

A. I slept with all the right people.

Q. If I called your boss, why would she say you were promoted so quickly?

A. She recognized real talent!

Q. Compare and contrast the best supervisor you have had, and the worst.

A. The best supervisor left me alone, never bothered me and definitely had very low expectations of me. The worst was one of those people who was enthusiastic, had high expectations and actually wanted to know what I was doing.

Q. Where would you place yourself on a continuum from being right-brained to left-brained?

A. Is the ability to know right from left a job requirement?

Q. Where do you see yourself on a continuum between being better at tactics or better at strategy?

A. My strategy has always been to leave the tactics to other people. I'm a big picture guy!

Q. Compare and contrast a typical day on your current job vs. an ideal day.

A. An ideal day and the word "job" don't mix at all.

Q. Imagine we've hired you, and you are having your one year performance review. What might your manager say about your work?

A. He would have quit out of frustration long before one year, so this is not a realistic scenario.

Q. What can you tell me about your creative ability?

A. I think my answers to most of your questions are pretty good indicators.

Q. I'd like to know how well you do as a problem solver.

A. Well, speaking of tough problems to solve … ever bet on the ponies?

Q. Tell me about you as a team player.

A. Teamwork is okay as long the other people don't get in my way.

Q. If you had a code failure, what would you do?

A. I am not sure what a code failure is but I can tell you that failure is not part of my vocabulary.

Q. Can you handle pressure?

A. I wouldn't know … no job has ever taxed my skills enough for me to find out.

Q. If you could live your life over again, what would you do differently?

A I would become a Personnel Manager so I could sit on that side of the table and ask the dumb questions.

Q. What are your hobbies?

A. Cockfighting, reading pornography, and polluting our rivers and oceans.

Q. Are you happy with your life?

A. Sure, other than the fact that I could stand to lose a few pounds … but you can obviously relate to that.

Off the Wall

Q. Why is a manhole cover round?

A. Because there is a noticeable lack of square-shaped men.

Q. How much water flows out of the Mississippi River every day?

A. A lot.

Q. How many gas stations are there in the United States?

A. With or without clean bathrooms?

Q. How many times does the average person say "the" in a day?

A. I'm sure thinking about this is a good use of my time!

Q. Do you have any fear that would deter you from traveling by air?

A. Yes. I worry about sitting next to someone who starts asking me stupid questions. I wouldn't be able to just get up and walk out—like I am right now.

Q. What is the most interesting trip you have ever taken?

A. I took a *lot* of interesting trips when I was in school at Berkeley during the sixties, so it would be hard to single out one as the best.

Q. If you could be any animal, which one would you be?

A. Let's see, you've already taken maggot, so how about Tse Tse fly?

Q. Are you willing to take a drug test as part of your employment?

A. Sure! What kind of drugs do I get to test?

Education

Q. Why did it take you six years to get your undergraduate degree?

A. Hey pal, you're lucky I got it at all!

Q. What was your major in college?

A. Pre-marital sex.

Q. How did you do in school?

A. I scored!

Q. Did your grade point average reflect your work ability?

A. Absolutely! Maximum results for minimum effort has always been my goal.

Q. Why didn't you do better in school?

A. What for? It's not as if I learned anything that has any practical value.

You Have *Got* To Be Kidding

Q. Do you consider yourself to be a smart person?

A. No. But I am the only person in the world with that opinion.

Q. Do you get bored doing the same work over and over again?

A. No. "The more boredom the better," is my motto. For example, if I were the Personnel Manager, I'd ask every prospective hiree the exact same questions.

Q. Tell me a story.

A. Once upon a time, there was this very boring man, but he thought he was clever. His job was to interview people for jobs. He asked the most ridiculous questions.

Q. Would you like to trade places with your boss?

A. You mean so I could act like an overbearing jerk?

Q. What would you do if it were your last day on earth?

A. Make sure that it's your last day as well.

Q. Can you name three of your biases?

A. Only three? Stupid people, ugly people and rap music.

Q. What is the most foolish thing you have ever done?

A. This is kind of embarrassing, but I caused that silly mix-up between the FBI and the Branch Davidians.

Q. Why did you apply for this job?

A. I got bored thinking of excuses for why I'm not working.

Q. What did you learn from your divorce?

A. How to recognize losers like you in less than 10 seconds.

Q. If you were a tree, what kind would you be?

A. The kind that dogs don't pee on.

Q. Have you ever contemplated suicide?

A. No, but if you keep asking me stupid questions I might consider it.

Q. Have you ever been so angry you wanted to kill someone?

A. How did you know what I was feeling?

Q. When do you plan on starting a family?

A. Is this some kind of a come-on?

Q. Describe the biggest crisis in your life.

A. Deciding whether or not to smack you.

Q. What is unique about you?

A. The fact that I have listened to your stupid questions longer than anyone else.

Q. Tell me about a time when strong fumes or odors affected your work. (Authors note: I swear I did not make this question up, but found it in a serious book! I hesitate to suggest a response, since the question itself is likely to be funnier. But since you insist, here goes.)

A. Are we talking about the cheese here?

Strengths & Weaknesses

Q. What do you consider to be some of your most outstanding qualities?

A. If you wouldn't mind moving to the couch, I'll show you.

Q. What is your greatest weakness?

A. Three-foot putts for par.

Q. What is your greatest strength?

A. I thrive on crisis and chaos. As a matter of fact, if there isn't enough crisis and chaos I create some just to strut my stuff.

Q. What is your greatest achievement?

A. Chugging four beers in under a minute!

Q. What kind of employee are you?

A. Depends on how much sleep I got the night before.

Q. Describe your personality.

A. Does the name “Sybil” mean anything to you?

Q. Have you ever failed?

A. No!

Q. Why have you had so many jobs?

A. Why not? Variety is the spice of life.

Q. How do you normally handle change?

A. I usually put it in a jar in my sock drawer.

Q. Do you consider yourself a success?

A. Of course. As you can see from my resumé, I've had more jobs than you.

Q. Name three personal characteristics that best describe you.

A. Tall, dark and handsome.

Q. Have you done the best work you are capable of?

A. No. I do the bare minimum to get by. Why do you ask?

Q. How do you normally handle criticism?

A. It depends on whether I have my gun with me or not.

Q. Why haven't you progressed more in your career?

A. I have been unfortunate in that I've worked for a bunch of losers like you.

Q. Why aren't you earning more money at your age?

A. See answer to previous question.

Q. In what ways are your qualifications unique or distinctive?

A. I thought you were supposed to recognize talent when you saw it.

Q. In what areas can others totally rely on your ability?

A. My co-workers can always rely on me to be a completely self-serving asshole.

Q. Rate yourself on a scale of one to ten.

A. You mean ten is as high as you go?

Dealing with the Boss

Q. What have you learned from your boss?

A. How to screw people with a smile on your face.

Q. How would you describe your boss's style?

A. He is too much of a slob to have anything described as "style."

Q. How do your work habits change when your boss is away?

A. I havc no work habits when my boss is away.

Q. What kind of supervisor gets the best results out of you?

A. The kind who are invisible. You know, neither seen nor heard.

Q. How would your boss describe your style?

A. If he could manage to string enough words together to form a sentence, he would probably say I'm a great guy.

Management Style

Q. How do you go about motivating others?

A. Cattle prods work nicely.

Q. Can you supervise people?

A. Sure. Tell people what to do, then kick their butts if they don't do it.

Q. Describe your management style.

A. Don't do anything you can make someone else do for you!

Q. How do you go about setting an example?

A. I never let anyone catch me sleeping in my office.

Q. What do you believe about the basic values of poor performers?

A. Does the term "thinning out the herd" mean anything to you?

Q. How do you know you are able to detect the "hot buttons" of others?

A. Usually by the volume of their moaning.

Q. How would your subordinates describe your management style?

A. Who cares!

Q. Describe how you have coordinated the work of subordinates who disliked one another.

A. I have them put on the gloves and whoever is left standing gets their way.

Team Player

Q. How do you normally relate to office politics?

A. I have a great time messing with people's heads, don't you?

Q. Are you a team player?

A. Of course! If you don't have a team, who are you going to manipulate?

Q. Do you prefer to work alone or with others?

A. I prefer to work with others but they always want me to work alone.

Q. Describe your style as a team player.

A. The total is the sum of the parts and I'm sure you know that "parts is parts."

Q. Describe your relationship with peers.

A. "They do what I tell them" pretty much sums it up.

Q. How do you handle conflict with peers?

A. They wouldn't dare.

Q. If someone is continuously critical of you and appears not to like you, what do you do?

A. Kick the crap out of them.

Q. Describe a healthy staff meeting you have been in.

A. Good cookies! The key to a good meeting is definitely proportional to the amount of free food.

Q. Describe an unhealthy staff meeting you have been in.

A. Well, there was that time Jim Jones and I couldn't agree on what flavor Kool-Aid to serve at the office party.

Q. Do you like to work with people?

A. Do you mean as opposed to working with animals or inanimate objects?

Q. When dealing with team members, how do you know if you are pushing too hard?

A. If there isn't blood, I haven't pushed too hard.

Q. What were the people like at your last company?

A. I hated them all, may they rest in peace.

Oral Communication Skills

Q. How do you know whether you're getting your point across to others?

A. If I don't have to slap the side of their heads more than once, I feel pretty certain they're listening.

Q. Describe a time when someone followed your instructions and got confused.

A. I gave a female visitor instructions to the restroom and she ended up in the men's room.

Q. How do you define a "problem person"?

A. Anyone who disagrees with me.

Q. How do you get new ideas accepted?

A. You mean my ideas could be rejected?

Q. Describe the toughest communication situation you have dealt with.

A. Giving my boss a status report when I have a hangover.

Q. When have you felt shy about communication?

A. When I was a teenager, I wrecked my dad's car. I guess you could say I was shy about discussing that with him.

Q. Describe a situation where your timing was good.

A. You mean like getting laryngitis so I didn't have to make that presentation?

Q. Are you a good communicator?

A. Huh?

Q. What have been your experiences making oral reports to management?

A. Waste of time. They ask a bunch of questions about stuff I don't know anything about.

Q. Timing is something that is very important in communicating … describe a situation where your timing was bad.

A. You mean like breaking up with my girlfriend after she told me she's pregnant?

Q. Tell me about a time you put your foot in your mouth.

A. Other than in this interview?

Q. How do you keep up with what is going on in the organization?

A. I hang out by the water cooler most of the day and shoot the breeze with whoever is around. I don't miss much!

Q. What does the term "two-way communication" mean to you?

A. That's easy: I speak and they listen.

Written Communication Skills

Q. What do you typically do with memos, bulletins, policy statements and so on?

A. Throw them away!

Q. Describe your experience in creating any form of written copy.

A. Does graffiti count?

Q. Have you ever used bulletin boards?

A. You mean like to sell an old car or something?

Q. How do you feel about your ability to write and spell in a written fashion?

A. I feel better about my ability to write and spell in an oral fashion.

Q. Have you written any memorable letters to customers?

A. You should have seen the one I wrote to the customer who swore at me on the phone. Boy did I show him a few new words!

Decision Making

Q. What types of decisions do you feel are beyond you?

A. Hey, if it requires more consideration than the flip of a coin, I leave it to the experts.

Q. In what types of situations do you think it is important for a manager to use democratic techniques in decision making?

A. Only after you have secretly made the decision but you are pretty certain they will vote in your direction anyway.

Q. Describe a situation where you have been part of the problem.

A. Oh, you're referring to the time I was a keynote speaker at the Cure Nymphomania conference. I can explain that.

Q. What types of decisions do you make without consulting your manager?

A. When to go to the bathroom, when to go to lunch and sometimes when to go home!

Q. Would you describe yourself as being more logical or more intuitive in solving problems?

A. Which would sound better to you?

Organizational Skills

Q. How do you schedule your time on unusually hectic days?

A. I don't! You mean some people do?

Q. How far ahead do you plan?

A. It depends on how creative I feel about generating excuses.

Q. Can you tell me about a time when your carefully laid plans were fouled up?

A. I could if I wanted to but I choose not to.

Q. What type of interruptions are good interruptions?

A. Like when my buddy calls in the middle of the day and wants to play golf?

Creativity

Q. What's the most creative thing you have ever done?

A. Concoct that resumé on your desk.

Q. Are you the type of person who likes to try new things?

A. My girlfriend seems to think so.

Q. What do you do that you consider to be a time-waster?

A. Go to work.

Q. As a young person, what types of activities were you involved in which would help you develop creative skills?

A. Lying to my parents. I came up with some real whoppers.

Q. Do you think everyone has the capacity to be creative?

A. Everyone except you.

Q. What types of situations allow you to demonstrate creativity in the workplace?

A. My creativity shines the brightest when I'm making up excuses for projects I didn't complete on time.

Q. What was the best idea you ever sold to your supervisor?

A. The time I convinced him to give me a raise I didn't deserve.

Ability to Deal With Stress

Q. How do you handle authority?

A. Attica! Attica!

Q. Have you ever felt overwhelmed by the responsibilities of your job?
A. Only during working hours.

Q. How did you react to the last rush situation you faced?
A. It's usually not a problem if you don't sweat the details.

Q. Describe a particularly difficult customer complaint you had to deal with.
A. A customer expected me to stop talking with my girlfriend on the phone and help him. Can you imagine the nerve?

Money

Q. How much money do you want?

A. How much do you have?

Q. What salary are you worth?

A. Double whatever you're making!

Q. Is money important to you?

A. What is this, a trick question?

Q. Are you motivated by money?

A. No, I am motivated by the things money can buy!

Sales

Q. What is your favorite closing tactic?

A. I have found crying to be quite effective.

Q. Do you give up on an account if you find out your chief competitor has gotten in there?

A. Absolutely! I feel that competition is very destructive and should be avoided at all costs. Don't you?

Q. When some salespeople get excited about closing a big sale, they sometimes accidentally offer the customer a little more than the company can comfortably deliver in order to clinch the sale. Has this ever happened to you?

A. You've never sold before, have you? When I get close to closing a big one I'll say anything!

Q. Describe a time when you faced unreasonable sales goals.

A. That implies that somewhere in history there has been a reasonable sales goal.

Q. At what level in an organization do you normally sell?

A. Low. I don't want to bother senior people.

Q. Sell me this pen.

A. Wow, if I can sell you a pen that's already yours, I guess I can fire you before I'm hired, right?

Q. Do you spend time licking your wounds after losing a big sale?

A. After I finish crying, I try to put up a good front with my family and co-workers but inside I'm just dying.

Miscellaneous

Q. How do you take direction?

A. I'm a man. I don't need any directions and I refuse to stop and get them.

Q. Wouldn't you feel more comfortable at another firm?

A. How did you know?

Q. Define cooperation.

A. Getting people to do what I want them to do, the way I want them to do it, when I want it done.

Q. What will you do if I don't hire you?

A. You don't want to know, so let's not tempt fate and even think about it.

Q. How much change is in your pocket/purse?

A. More than you make in a month, why?

Q. What mistake might we make in hiring you?

A. What mistake wouldn't you make if you hire me?

Q. You're walking down a path and come to a fork in the road, with a lake in one direction and a forest in the other. Which direction do you choose?

A. You are one sick puppy!

Q. Do something that will infuriate me.

A. You mean like compare my IQ to yours?

Q. What do you need to be a happy human being?

A. Fast cars, fast food, and fast women. Not necessarily in that order.

Q. Describe your perfect job.

A. Sitting on the beach in Hawaii judging a bikini contest and getting paid really big money for doing so.

Q. What section of the newspaper do you turn to first?

A. The obituaries.

Q. What is the worst thing you have heard about this organization?

A. Everyone told me that you ask really stupid questions during interviews and I just had to see for myself.

Q. Can we check your references?

A. Only if I can check yours.

Q. How soon can you start?

A. Well, I am scheduled to sell—I mean, *donate* blood this afternoon, so how does tomorrow sound?

Q. Have you ever worked swing shifts?

A. Hey pal, my sex life is none or your business!

Q. How would you rate me as an interviewer?

A. The worst!!

For more information about
Selecting Winners, Inc. products and
services, or to inquire about having
Barry Shamis speak for your group,
please contact us at:

Selecting Winners Inc.
210 - 209th Place SE
Redmond, WA 98053

1-800-994-4946
Fax: 1-206-313-4665
bshamis@selwin.com